emergency compliment

Megs Senk

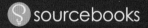

Published by Sourcebooks, Inc.
P.O. Box 4410, Naperville, Illinois 60567-4410
(630) 961-3900
Fax: (630) 961-2168
www.sourcebooks.com

Printed and bound in China.
LEO 10 9 8 7 6 5 4 3 2 1

To anyone who is really needing
a book dedicated to them today.

Your 2nd grade teacher thought you had the best penmanship

If you ordered anchovy pizza, everyone would eat it without complaining

You look breathtaking in fluorescent lighting

Your dance skills make babies gasp and eagles soar

That person behind you at the concert thought your hair smelled "magical"

Thanks to jerks, breakups, bad hair days, failed tests, butt dials, awkward sunburns, and the many other awful things in life—without which, this book would have never been possible.

but also to:

John Senk, whose snores have the fortitude to shake a house's foundation.
Rose Senk, who has perfected the art of blinking in photos.
Julie Senk, who has managed to be viewed as a cool and respectable adult despite her obsession with sharks and ghosts.
wk12.8, whose unique blend of annoyance and brilliance inspired this book.

Megs Senk is an art director who is commonly grumpy,
so it's kinda funny that she wrote a book of compliments.

You're listed as a "favorite" in 80% of your friends' phones

You have the lower body strength and confidence to ride a tandem bike solo

You could probably just walk into Mordor

Once the delivery guys played Rock, Paper, Scissors to determine who brought your pizza

Spiders are DEFINITELY more scared of you than you are of them

No one at the karaoke bar wants to be the act to follow you

Your spirit animal is probably a cool, obscure one from *National Geographic*

Your parents brag about you to their first and second cousins

You still have the highest score on that arcade game in your hometown

Your coworker finds the sound of you typing an email to be extremely soothing

The person in
the car next to
you really wanted
that red light to
last longer

That dude on
the street thought
you killed that
parking job

Your walk can best be described as a "sophisticated yet relatable strut"

The cashier at the grocery store thought your produce selection was inspired

Everyone thought that coffee stain on your shirt was just some cool European fabric pattern

Your pronunciation of "pecan" is the correct pronunciation

You are always one of the best-smelling people at the gym

The accounting department equates your expense reports to Victorian poetry

Your best friend's mom always talks about how you are a "great influence"

You are exactly the right height

When you messed up the punch line, it actually made the joke

The IT department is always impressed with the originality of your passwords

I don't know how old you are, but you definitely look great for that age

Your hugs are a more legitimate source of energy than a 16 oz. coffee

**Trust me,
this is the best
your elbows
have ever looked**

Construction workers respect you too much to whistle at you

A DMV employee brought your license photo to their hairdresser

Your Band-Aids stay on 67% longer than the average person's

You deserve every high five that comes your way

Your selfies have been described as introspective, daring, and hot

You are one of six people in the world that get IKEA furniture instructions right on the first try

TSA agents always covet your shoe selection

Your smile is as contagious as the flu, but with less vomiting

You have an uncanny ability to select the most interesting combination of movie snacks

Road trip buddies always appreciate how small your bladder is

Much like ChapStick, you are not medically necessary but still quite addictive

The lead singer was singing to you...or the person directly next to you. Definitely one of you two

Your first kiss thought it was like your fourth or fifth kiss

Your favorite sports team really thinks you have what it takes to be their water boy/girl

Your shower would like to nominate you for a Grammy. But it can't because it's a shower

The barista at your local Starbucks only misspelled your name the first five times you ordered from them

You are the only one your friends trust to efficiently divide up the dinner bill

At least seven people would join you in dancing the Electric Slide at a wedding

People are deeply honored when you ask them to help you move

You are totally capable of keeping a cactus alive for two-three weeks

No one ever questions whether you wash your hands before leaving the bathroom

Someone out there has the same irrational fears about sharks and choking on Jell-O as you

If and when aliens abduct you, they are going to treat you so well

Dolphins want to swim with you and also think you have impeccable taste in swimwear

Mosquitoes and vampires reserve your blood for special occasions

85% of your blind dates immediately regret not wearing a nicer outfit after meeting you

The squirrel that's always in the tree near your window yearns to be your pet

You drink just the right amount of water

Your search history is pretty tame, considering

But seriously, you're great—you should know that